MW01223286

Evangelical Catechism

The Evangelical Catechism

Published by
Authority
of the
Evangelical Synod
of North America

UNITED CHURCH PRESS
Cleveland, Ohio

United Church Press
Cleveland, Ohio 44115

Copyright © renewed 1957
Eden Publishing House

Copyright acquired 1985
by United Church Press

99   10 9 8 7 6

ISBN 0-8298-0761-6

Contents

ESSENTIALS OF THE CATECHISM

The Apostles' Creed

I believe in God the Father Almighty, Maker of heaven and earth:

And in Jesus Christ, his only begotten Son, our Lord: who was conceived by the Holy Spirit, born of the Virgin Mary; suffered under Pontius Pilate, was crucified, dead, and buried; he descended into hell; the third day he rose again from the dead; he ascended into heaven, and sitteth at the right hand of God the Father Almighty; from thence he shall come to judge the quick and the dead.

I believe in the Holy Spirit; the one holy universal Christian Church; the communion of saints; the forgiveness of sins; the resurrection of the body; and the life everlasting. Amen.

THE SUMMARY OF THE FIRST ARTICLE

I believe that God has made me and all creatures; that he has given me and still preserves my body and soul, eyes, ears, and all my members, my reason and all my senses, also food and clothing, home and family, and all my possessions; that he daily and abundantly provides me with all the necessaries of life, protects and preserves me from all danger; and all this he does out of sheer fatherly and divine goodness and mercy, without any merit or worthiness on my part. For all this I am in duty bound to think, praise, serve, and obey him. This is most certainly true.

THE SUMMARY OF THE SECOND ARTICLE

I believe that Jesus Christ—true God, begotten of the Father from eternity, and also true man, born of the Virgin Mary—is my Lord, who has redeemed, purchased, and delivered me, a lost and condemned creature, from all sins, from death, and from the power of satan, not with silver or gold, but with his holy, precious blood and with his innocent suffering and death; that I may be his own, live under him in his Kingdom, and serve him in everlasting righteousness, innocence, and blessedness; even as he is risen from the dead, lives and reigns to all eternity.

This is most certainly true.

THE SUMMARY OF THE THIRD ARTICLE

I believe that I can not by my own reason or strength believe in my Lord Jesus Christ, or come to him; but the Holy Spirit has called me by the Gospel, enlightened me with his gifts, sanctified and preserved me in the true faith; even as he calls, gathers, enlightens, and preserves the whole Christian Church on earth and keeps it with Jesus Christ in the one true faith; in which Christian Church he daily and abundantly forgives me and all believers all sins, and on the last day will raise up me and all the dead, and will give unto me and all believers in Christ everlasting life.

This is most certainly true.

The Ten Commandments
(Exodus 20:1-17)

I

"I am the LORD your God, who brought you out of the land of Egypt, out of the house of bondage.
"You shall have no other gods before me."

II

"You shall not make yourself a graven image, or any likeness of anything that is in heaven above, or that is in the earth beneath, or that is in the water under the earth; you shall not bow down to them or serve them; for I the LORD your God am a jealous God, visiting the iniquity of the fathers upon the children to the third and the fourth generation of those who hate me, but showing steadfast love to thousands of those who love me and keep my commandments."

III

"You shall not take the name of the LORD your God in vain; for the LORD will not hold him guiltless who takes his name in vain."

IV

"Remember the sabbath day, to keep it holy. Six days you shall labor, and do all your work; but the seventh day is a sabbath to the LORD your God; in it you shall not do any work, you, or your son, or your daughter, your manservant, or your maidservant, or your cattle, or the sojourner who is within your gates; for in six days the Lord made heaven and earth, the sea, and all that is in them, and rested the seventh day; therefore the Lord blessed the sabbath day and hallowed it."

V

"Honor your father and your mother, that your days may be long in the land which the Lord your God gives you."

VI

"You shall not kill."

VII

"You shall not commit adultery."

VIII

"You shall not steal."

IX

"You shall not bear false witness against your neighbor."

X

"You shall not covet your neighbor's house; you shall not covet your neighbor's wife, or his manservant, or his maidservant, or his ox, or his ass, or anything that is your neighbor's."

The Summary of the Ten Commandments

"You shall love the Lord your God with all your heart, and with all your soul, and with all your might." (Deut. 6:5.) "You shall love your neighbor as yourself." (Lev. 19:18.) "On these two commandments depend all the law and the prophets." (Matt. 22:40.)

God says: " 'Cursed be he who does not confirm the words of this law by doing them.' " (Deut. 27:26; Gal. 3:10.) "You shall therefore keep my statues and my ordinances, by doing which a man shall live: I am the Lord." (Lev. 18:5; Luke 10:28.)

The Beatitudes

"Blessed are the poor in spirit, for theirs is the kingdom of heaven.

"Blessed are those who mourn, for they shall be comforted.

"Blessed are the meek, for they shall inherit the earth.

"Blessed are those who hunger and thirst for righteousness, for they shall be satisfied.

"Blessed are the merciful, for they shall obtain mercy.

"Blessed are the pure in heart, for they shall see God.

"Blessed are the peacemakers, for they shall be called sons of God.

"Blessed are those who are persecuted for righteousness' sake, for theirs is the kingdom of heaven."   (Matthew 5:3-10.)

The Lord's Prayer

"Our Father who art in heaven, Hallowed be thy name. Thy kingdom come, They will be done, On earth as it is in heaven. Give us this day our daily bread; And forgive us our debts, As we also have forgiven our debtors; And lead us not into temptation, But deliver us from evil." *For thine is the kingdom, and the power, and the glory, forever. Amen.* (Matthew 6:9-13.)

The Institution of Holy Baptism

Matt. 28:18-20: "All authority in heaven and on earth has been given to me. Go therefore and make disciples of all nations, baptizing them in the name of the Father and of the Son and of the Holy Spirit, teaching them to observe all that I have commanded you; and lo, I am with you always, to the close of the age."

The Institution of the Lord's Supper

The Lord Jesus on the night when he was betrayed took bread, and when he had given thanks, he broke it, and gave it to the disciples and said, "Take, eat; this is my body which is for you. Do this in remembrance of me."

In the same way also he took a cup, after supper, and when he had given thanks he gave it to them, saying, "Drink of it, all of you; for this is my blood of the covenant, which is poured out for many for the forgiveness of sins. Do this, as often as you drink it, in remembrance of me." (Matt. 26:26-28; Mark 14:22-24; Luke 22:19-20; 1 Cor. 11:23-25.)

THE BOOKS OF THE BIBLE

The Old Testament (39 Books)

HISTORICAL BOOKS (17)

Genesis	Ruth
Exodus	1 and 2 Samuel
Leviticus	1 and 2 Kings
Numbers	1 and 2 Chronicles
Deuteronomy	Ezra
Joshua	Nehemiah
Judges	Esther

POETICAL BOOKS (5)

Job	Ecclesiastes
Psalms	Song of Solomon
Proverbs	

PROPHETICAL BOOKS (17)

a. THE GREATER PROPEHTS

Isaiah	Ezekiel
Jeremiah	Daniel
Lamentations	

b. THE LESSER PROPHETS

Hosea	Jonah	Zephaniah
Joel	Micah	Haggai
Amos	Nahum	Zechariah
Obediah	Habakkuk	Malachi

The New Testament (27 Books)

HISTORICAL BOOKS (5)

Matthew	Luke	The Acts
Mark	John	

DOCTRINAL BOOKS (The 21 Epistles)

a. The Epistles of St. Paul (13)

Romans	Colossians
1 and 2 Corinthians	1 and 2 Thessalonians
Galatians	1 and 2 Timothy
Ephesians	Titus
Philippians	Philemon

b. The Epistle to the Hebrews

c. The Seven General Epistles

James	1, 2 and 3 John
1 and 2 Peter	Jude

PROPHETIC

The Revelation of St. John

INTRODUCTION

1. What should be the chief concern of man?

Man's chief concern should be to seek after the Kingdom of God and his righteousness.

Matt. 6:33, "But seek first his kingdom and his righteousness, and all these things shall be yours as well."

Matt. 16:26. "For what will it profit a man, if he gains the whole world and forfeits his life? Or what shall a man give in return for his life?"

2. How do we obtain righteousness?

We obtain righteousness through faith in our Lord Jesus Christ, by whom we are saved.

Acts 16:31. "Believe in the Lord Jesus, and you will be saved, you and your household."

3. What then must we do to be saved?

We must believe on the Lord Jesus Christ.

John 6:40. "For this is the will of my Father, that every one who sees the Son and believes in him should have eternal life; and I will raise him up at the last day."

4. Where are we told what we must do to be saved?

God has told us what we must do to be saved in his Word, the Holy Bible, which was written by men who were moved by the Holy Spirit.

2 Peter. 1:21. Because no prophecy ever came by the impulse of man, but men moved by the Holy Spirit spoke from God.

2 Tim. 3:15-17. And how from childhood you have been acquainted with the sacred writings which you are able to instruct you for salvation through faith in Christ Jesus. All scripture is inspired by God and profitable for teaching, for reproof, for correction, and for training in righteousness, that the man of God may be complete, equipped for every good work.

Ps. 119:105. The word is a lamp to my feet and a light to my path.

5. In what two ways has God in the Bible revealed his will toward man?

In the Bible God has revealed his will toward man by the Law and by the Gospel.

PART I
GOD AND HIS ATTRIBUTES

6. What has God revealed about himself in the Bible?

In the Bible God has revealed to us that he is One God, that he is Spirit, and that he is Life, Light, and Love.

Deut. 6:4. "Hear, O Israel: The Lord our God is one Lord."

John 4:24. "God is spirit, and those who worship him must worship in spirit and truth."

1 John 5:20. This is the true God and eternal life.

1 John 1:5. God is light and in him is no darkness at all.

1 John 4:8. God is love.

7. What do we mean when we say: God is Life?

"God is Life" means that he is eternal, un-changeable, and ever present.

God is eternal:

Ps. 90:1-2. Lord, thou hast been our dwelling place in all generations. Before the mountains were brought forth, or ever thou hadst formed the earth and the world, from everlasting to everlasting thou art God.

Rev. 1:8. "I am the Alpha and the Omega," says the Lord God, who is and who was and who is to come, the Almighty.

Isa. 26:4. "Trust in the Lord for ever, for the Lord God is an everlasting rock."

Unchangeable:

Mal. 3:6. "For I the LORD do not change."

Jas. 1:17. Every good endowment and every perfect gift is from above, coming down from the Father of lights with whom there is no variation or shadow due to change.

Ever present:

Jer. 23:23-24. "Am I a God at hand, says the LORD, and not a God afar off? Can a man hide himself in secret places so that I cannot see him? says the LORD. Do I not fill heaven and earth? says the LORD."

Acts 17:27-28. "Yet he is not far from each of us, for 'In him we live and move and have our being.'"

Ps. 139:7-10. Whither shall I go from thy Spirit? Or whither shall I flee from thy presence? If I ascend to heaven, thou art there! If I make my bed in Sheol, thou art there! If I take the wings of the morning and dwell in the uttermost parts of the sea, even there thy hand shall lead me, and thy right hand shall hold me.

Ps. 23:4. Even though I walk through the valley of the shadow of death, I fear no evil; for thou art with me; thy rod and thy staff, they comfort me.

8. What do we mean when we say that God is Light?

"God is Light" means that he is true, all-knowing, all-wise, holy, almighty, and just.

God is true:

Num. 23:19. "God is not man, that he should lie, or a son of man, that he should repent. Has he said, and will he not do it? Or has he spoken, and will he not fulfill it?"

1 John 5:10. He who believes in the Son of God has the testimony in himself. He who does not believe God, has made him a liar, because he has not believed in the testimony that God has borne to his Son.

Ps. 119:89-90. For ever, O LORD, thy word is firmly fixed in the heavens. Thy faithfulness endures to all generations.

All-knowing:

Ps. 139:1-4. O LORD, thou hast searched me and known me! Thou knowest when I sit down and when I rise up; thou discernest my thoughts from afar. Thou searchest out my path and my lying down, and art acquainted with all my ways. Even before a word is on my tongue, lo, O LORD, thou knowest it altogether.

1 Sam. 16:7. "For man looks on the outward appearance, but the LORD looks on the heart."

Matt. 6:8. "For your Father knows what you need before you ask him."

All-wise:

Isa. 55:8-9. "For my thoughts are not your thoughts, neither are your ways my ways, says the LORD. For as the heavens are higher than the earth, so are my ways higher than your ways and my thoughts than your thoughts."

Ps. 104:24. O LORD, how manifold are thy works! In wisdom has thou made them all; the earth is full of thy creatures.

Rom. 8:28. We know that in everything God works for good with those who love him.

1 Pet. 5:7. Cast all your anxieties on him, for he cares about you.

Jas. 1:5. If any of you lacks wisdom, let him ask God who gives to all men generously and without reproaching.

Holy:

Lev. 19:2. "You shall be holy; for I the LORD your God am holy."

Isa. 6:3. "Holy, holy, holy is the LORD of hosts; the whole earth is full of his glory."

Rev. 15:4. "Who shall not fear and glorify thy name, O LORD? For thou alone art holy. All nations shall come and worship thee, for thy judgments have been revealed."

1 Pet. 1:15-16. But as he who called you is holy, be holy yourselves in all your conduct; since it is written, "You shall be holy, for I am holy."

Almighty:

Gen. 17:1. "I am God Almighty; walk before me, and be blameless."

Luke 1:37. "For with God nothing will be impossible."

Ps. 33:8-9. Let all the earth fear the LORD, let all the inhabitants of the world stand in awe of him! For he spoke, and it came to be; he commanded, and it stood forth.

Isa. 40:26. Lift up your eyes on high and see: who created these? He who brings out their host by number, calling them all by name; by the greatness of his might, and because he is strong in power not one is missing.

Just:

Ps. 14:17. The LORD is just in all his ways, and kind in all his doings.

Ps. 5:4. The LORD works vindication and justice for all who are oppressed.

Ps. 5:4. For thou art not a God who delights in wickedness; evil may not sojourn with thee.

Rom. 2:6. For he will render to every man according to his works.

Is. 41:10. Fear not, for I am with you, be not dismayed, for I am your God; I will strengthen you, I will help you, I will uphold you with my victorious right hand.

Ps. 37:25. I have been young, and now am old, yet I have not seen the righteous forsaken or his children begging bread.

9. What do we mean when we say: God is Love?

"God is Love" means that he is blessed, good, gracious, and merciful.

God is blessed:

1 Tim. 6:15-16. And this will be made manifest at the proper time by the blessed and only Sovereign, the King of kings and Lord of lords, who alone has immortality and dwells in unapproachable light, whom no man has ever seen or can see. To him be honor and eternal dominion. Amen.

Good:

Ps 145:9. The LORD is good to all, and his compassion is over all that he has made.

Ps. 107:1. O give thanks to the LORD, for he is good; for his steadfast love endures for ever!

Ps. 36:5. Thy steadfast love, O LORD, extends to the heavens, thy faithfulness to the clouds.

Gracious and merciful:

Ps. 103:8-10. The LORD is merciful and gracious, slow to anger and abounding in steadfast love. He will not always chide, nor will he keep his anger for ever. He does not deal with us according to our sins, nor requite us according to our iniquities.

Ps. 103:13. As a father pities his children, so the LORD pities those who fear him.

Ps. 103: 17-18. But the steadfast love of the LORD is from everlasting to everlasting upon those who fear him, and his righteousness to children's children, to those who keep his covenant and remember to do his commandments.

Lam. 3: 22-23. The steadfast love of the LORD never ceases, his mercies never come to an end; they are new every morning; great is thy faithfulness.

2 Chron. 30:9. "For the LORD your God is gracious and merciful, and will not turn away his face from you, if you return to him."

Luke 6:36. "Be merciful, even as your Father is merciful."

10. What mystery concerning God does the Bible reveal?

The Bible reveals to us the mystery that in the one God there are three persons, the Father, the Son, and the Holy Spirit, and that these three are one.

Matt. 28:19. "Go therefore and make disciples of all nations, baptizing them in the name of the Father and of the Son and of the Holy Spirit."

2 Cor. 13:14. The grace of the Lord Jesus Christ and the love of God and the fellowship of the Holy Spirit be with you all.

Matt. 3:16-17. And when Jesus was baptized, he went up immediately from the water, and behold, the heavens were opened and he saw the Spirit of God descending like a dove, and alighting on him; and lo, a voice from heaven, saying, "This is my beloved Son, with whom I am well pleased."

Num. 6:24-26. "The LORD bless you and keep you: The LORD make his face to shine upon you, and be gracious to you: The LORD lift up his countenance upon you, and give you peace."

PART II

THE THREE ARTICLES OF THE CHRISTIAN FAITH

11. In what creed does the Christian Church confess its faith in the Triune God?

The Christian Church confesses its faith in the Triune God in the Apostles' Creed.

THE APOSTLES' CREED

I believe in God the Father Almighty, Maker of heaven and earth:

And in Jesus Christ, his only begotten Son, our Lord: who was conceived by the Holy Spirit, born of the Virgin Mary; suffered under Pontius Pilate: was crucified, dead, and buried; he descended into hell; the third day he rose again from the dead; he ascended into heaven, and sitteth at the right hand of God the Father Almighty; from thence he shall come to judge the quick and the dead.

I believe in the Holy Spirit; the one holy universal Christian Church; the communion of saints; the forgiveness of sins; the resurrection of the body; and the life everlasting. Amen.

The First Article of the Christian Faith

12. What is the First Article of the Christian Faith?

I believe in God the Father Almighty, Maker of heaven and earth.

13. Of what does the First Article of the Christian
Faith treat?

The First Article of the Christian Faith treats of God the Father and of the work of creation.

14. What do we mean when we say, "God the Father
Almighty, Maker of heaven and earth"?

In the beginning God created heaven and earth by the power of his Word.

Gen. 1:1. In the beginning God created the heavens
and the earth.

Ps. 33:6. By the word of the LORD the heavens were
made, and all their host by the breath of his mouth.

Heb. 11:3. By faith we understand that the world was
created by the word of God, so that what is seen was
made out of things which do not appear.

15. How does God constantly prove himself to be the
Creator?

God constantly proves himself to be the Creator by his fatherly providence, whereby he preserves and governs all things.

Gen. 8:22. "While the earth remains, seedtime and
harvest, cold and heat, summer and winter, day and night,
shall not cease."

Ps. 145:15-16. The eyes of all look to thee, and thou
givest them their food in due season. Thou openest thy
hand, thou satisfiest the desire of every living thing.

Deut. 8:10. "And you shall eat and be full, and you
shall bless the LORD your God for the good land he has
given you."

Matt. 6:25. "Therefore I tell you, do not be anxious
about your life, what you shall eat or what you shall
drink, nor about your body, what you shall put on. Is not
life more than food, and the body more than clothing?"

Ps. 121:3-4. He will not let your foot be moved, he who keeps you will not slumber. Behold, he who keeps Israel will neither slumber nor sleep.

Gen. 50:20. "As for you, you meant evil against me; but God meant it for good, to bring it about that many people should be kept alive, as they are today."

Prov. 16:9. A man's mind plans his way, but the LORD directs his steps.

16. What has God done for you?

I believe that God has made me and all creatures; that he has given me and still preserves my body and soul, eyes, ears, and all my members, my reason and all my senses, also food and clothing, home and family, and all my possessions.

17. What does God still do for you?

God daily and abundantly provides me with all the necessaries of life, protects and preserves me from all danger.

18. Why does God do this for you?

God does all this out of sheer fatherly and divine goodness and mercy, without any merit or worthiness on my part.

19. What do you owe God for all this?

For all this I am in duty bound to thank, praise, serve, and obey him.

20. What are the angels?

The angels are ministering spirits who are sent forth by God to do his will.

Ps. 103:20. Bless the LORD, O you his angels, you mighty ones who do his word.

Heb. 1:14. Are they not all ministering spirits sent forth to serve, for the sake of those who are to obtain salvation?

Ps. 91:11-12. For he will give his angels charge of you to guard you in all your ways. On their hands they will bear you, lest you dash your foot against a stone.

Ps. 34:7. The angel of the LORD encamps around those who fear him, and delivers them.

Luke 15:10. "Even so, I tell you, there is joy before the angels of God over one sinner who repents."

21. Have all the angels always obeyed the will of God?

No; for many of the angels once sinned against God and were banished to hell as enemies of God and man. The chief among the evil spirits is called the devil, or satan.

2 Pet. 2:4. God did not spare the angels when they sinned, but cast them into hell and committed them to pits of nether gloom to be kept until the judgment.

Eph. 6:12. For we are not contending against flesh and blood, but against the principalities, against the powers, against the world rulers of this present darkness, against the spiritual hosts of wickedness in the heavenly places.

1 Pet. 5:8. Be sober, be watchful. Your adversary the devil prowls around like a roaring lion, seeking some one to devour.

Jas. 4:7. Resist the devil and he will flee from you.

22. What is the principal creature on earth?

The principal creature on earth is man, created in the image of God, so that we could know him and live in blessed fellowship with him.

Gen. 1:27. So God created man in his own image, in the image of God he created him; male and female he created them.

Gen. 1:31. And God saw everything that he had made, and behold, it was very good.

23. Did man remain as he was created?

No; for our first parents fell away from God when they permitted satan to lead them into unbelief and disobedience.

Read Genesis 3.

24. What were the sad consequences of this fall of man?

By this fall man lost the strength and beauty of God's image and came under the power of satan, sin, and death. This corruption has been transmitted from Adam to all mankind.

Gen. 2:17. "But of the tree of the knowledge of good and evil you shall not eat, for in the day that you eat of it you shall die."

Gen. 3:17-19. "Because you have listened to the voice of your wife, and have eaten of the tree of which I commanded you, 'You shall not eat of it,' cursed is the ground because of you; in toil you shall eat of it all the days of your life; thorns and thistles it shall bring forth to you; and you shall eat the plants of the field. In the sweat of your face you shall eat bread till you return to the ground, for out of it you were taken; you are dust, and to dust you shall return."

Rom. 5:12. Therefore as sin came into the world through one man and death through sin, and so death spread to all men because all men sinned.

Rom. 7:14. We know that the law is spiritual! but I am carnal, sold under sin.

1 John 3:8. He who commits sin is of the devil; for the devil has sinned from the beginning. The reason the Son of God appeared was to destroy the words of the devil.

25. What is man's condition since the fall?

Since the fall, man is not prepared to do good, but inclined to do evil. This inherited corruption is called original sin.

Gen. 8:21. "For the imagination of man's heart is evil from his youth."

John 3:6. "That which is born of the flesh is flesh, and that which is born of the Spirit is spirit."

1 John 1:8. If we say we have no sin, we deceive ourselves, and the truth is not in us.

26. What is sin?

Sin is unbelief and disobedience in thought and desire, word and deed, whereby evil is done or good is neglected, whether thoughtlessly or wilfully.

Ps. 19:12. But who can discern his errors? clear thou me from hidden faults.

Matt. 15:18. But what comes out of the mouth proceeds from the heart, and this defiles a man.

Jas. 4:17. Whoever knows what is right to do and fails to do it, for him it is sin.

Luke 12:47. "And that servant who knew his master's will, but did not make ready or act according to his will, shall receive a severe beating."

1 Tim. 5:22. Do not be hasty in the laying on of hands, nor participate in another man's sins; keep yourself pure.

27. What is the punishment of sin?

The punishment of sin is death, as it is written Romans 6:23: The wages of sin is death.

28. How manifold is this death?

This death is threefold: physical, spiritual, and eternal.

Ps. 90:7-8. For we are consumed by thy anger; by thy wrath we are overwhelmed. Thou hast set our iniquities before thee, our secret sins in the light of thy contenance.

Matt. 10:28. "And do not fear those who kill the body but cannot kill the soul; rather fear him who can destroy both soul and body in hell."

Matt. 25:41. " 'Depart from me, you cursed, into the eternal fire prepared for the devil and his angels.' "

Eph. 2:1. And you he made alive, when you were dead through the trespasses and sins.

29. What did God in his mercy resolve to do to save mankind from sin and its punishment?

God in his mercy resolved from all eternity to save fallen mankind through his only begotten Son.

2 Tim. 1:9. Who saved us and called us with a holy calling, not in virture of our works but in virtue of his own purpose and the grace which he gave us in Christ Jesus ages ago.

30. How did God prepare mankind for the coming of the Saviour?

God prepared mankind for the coming of the Saviour by the promises given in Paradise and to the patriarchs of Israel, by the Law delivered to Moses, by forms of worship in the Old Covenant, and by the preaching of the prophets.

Gen. 3:15. "I will put enmity between you and the woman, and between your seed and her seed; he shall bruise your head, and you shall bruise his heel."

Gen. 22:18. "And by your descendants shall all the nations of the earth bless themselves."

Gen. 49:10. "The scepter shall not depart from Judah, nor the ruler's staff from between his feet, until he comes to whom it belongs; and to him shall be the obedience of the peoples."

Jer. 33:15-16. "In those days and at that time I will cause a righteous Branch to spring forth for David; and he shall execute justice and righteousness in the land. In those days Judah will be saved and Jerusalem will dwell securely. And this is the name by which it will be called: "The LORD is our righteousness.' "

Mic. 5:2. But you, O Bethlehem Ephrathah, who are little to be among the clans of Judah, from you shall come forth for me one who is to be ruler in Israel, whose origin is from of old, from ancient days.

Isa. 9:6. For to us a child is born, to us a son is given; and the government will be upon his shoulder, and his name will be called "Wonderful Counselor, Mighty God, Everlasting Father, Prince of Peace."

Acts 10:43. "To him all the prophets bear witness that every one who believes in him receives forgiveness of sins through his name."

Gal. 3:24. So that the law was our custodian until Christ came, that we might be justified by faith.

The Law of God

31. Where do we find the law of God in brief form?

We find the law of God briefly given in the Ten Commandments.

(Exod. 20:1-17; Deut. 5:6-21.)

32. What is the First Commandment?

"I am the LORD your God, who brought you out of the land of Egypt, out of the house of bondage. "You shall have no other gods before me."

33. What is meant by the First Commandment?

God forbids all idolatry and requires that we fear, love, and trust in him above all things.

Matt. 4:10. "You shall worship the Lord your God and him only shall you serve." (Deut. 6:13.)

1 John 2:15. Do not love the world or the things in the world. If any one loves the world, love for the Father is not in him.

Matt. 10:37. "He who loves father or mother more than me is not worthy of me; and he who loves son or daughter more than me is not worthy of me."

Jer. 17:5. Thus says the LORD: "Cursed is the man who trusts in man and makes flesh his arm, whose heart turns away from the LORD."

Eccles. 12:13. The end of the matter; all has been heard. Fear God, and keep his commandments; for this is the whole duty of man.

1 John 5:3. For this is the love of God, that we keep his commandments. And his commandments are not burdensome.

Ps. 37:5. Commit your ways to the LORD; trust in him, and he will act.

Prov. 3:5. Trust in the LORD with all your heart, and do not rely on your own insight.

34. What is the Second Commandment?

"You shall not make yourself a graven image or any likeness of anything that is in heaven above, or that is in the earth beneath, or that is in the water under the earth; you shall not bow down to them or serve them; for I the LORD your God am a jealous God, visiting the iniquity of the father upon the children to the third and the fourth generation of those who hate me, but showing steadfast love to thousands of those who love me and keep my commandments."

35. What is meant by the Second Commandment?

God forbids us to worship him in any image; He requires us to worship him as he has taught us in his Word and revealed himself to us in his Son Jesus Christ.

Isa. 42:8. "I am the LORD, that is my name; my glory I give to no other, nor my praise to graven images."

Isa. 40:18. To whom then will you liken God, or what likeness compare with him?

John 1:18. No one has ever seen God; the only Son, who is in the bosom of the Father, he has made him known.

John 4:24. "God is spirit, and those who worship him must worship in spirit and truth."

36. What is the Third Commandment?

"You shall not take the name of the LORD your God in vain; for the LORD will not hold him guiltless who takes his name in vain."

37. What is meant by the Third Commandment?

God forbids that we profane or abuse his name by cursing, false swearing, witchcraft, or unnecessary oaths, and requires that we use his holy name with fear and reverence.

Jas. 3:10. From the same mouth come blessing and cursing. My brethen, this ought not to be so.

Lev. 19:12. "And you shall not swear by my name falsely, and so profane the name of your God: I am the LORD."

Rom. 10:13. For, "every one who calls upon the name of the Lord will be saved."

Ps. 50:15. "And call upon me in the day of trouble; I will deliver you, and you shall glorify me."

Matt. 10:32-33. "So every one who acknowledges me before men, I also will acknowledge before my Father who is in heaven; but whoever denies me before men, I also will deny before my Father who is in heaven."

Ps. 92:1. It is good to give thanks to the LORD, to sing praises to thy name, O Most High.

38. What is the Fourth Commandment?

"Remember the sabbath day, to keep it holy. Six days you shall labor, and do all your work; but the seventh day is a sabbath to the LORD your God; in it you shall not do any work, you, or your son, or your daughter, your manservant, or

your maidservant, or your cattle, or the sojourner
who is within your gates; for in six days the
LORD made heaven and earth, the sea, and all that
is in them, and rested the seventh day; therefore
the LORD blessed the sabbath day and hallowed it."

39. What is meant by the Fourth Commandment?

God requires that we hallow the Lord's Day
by resting from wordly employment, by diligently
going to church, and by using the day for the welfare of ourselves and others, and thus to the
honor of God.

Ezek. 20:20. "Hallow my sabbaths that they may be a
sign between me and you, that you may know that I the
LORD am your God."

Col. 3:16-17. Let the word of Christ dwell in you
richly, as you teach and admonish one another in all wisdom, and as you sing psalms and hymns and spiritual
songs with thankfulness in your hearts to God. And whatever you do, in word or deed, do everything in the name of
the Lord Jesus, giving thanks to God the Father through
him.

Ps. 26:6-8. I wash my hands in innocence, and go
about thy altar, O LORD, singing aloud a song of thanksgiving, and telling all thy wondrous deeds. O LORD, I love
the habitation of thy house, and the place where thy glory
dwells.

Heb. 10:25. Not neglecting to meet together, as is the
habit of some.

Eccles. 5:1. Guard your steps when you go to the
house of God; to draw near to listen is better than to offer
the sacrifice of fools; for they do not know that they are
doing evil.

Luke 11:28. "Blessed rather are those who hear the word of God and keep it!"

Exod. 20:24. " 'In every place where I cause my name to be remembered I will come to you and bless you.' "

40. What is the Fifth Commandment?

"Honor your father and your mother, that your days may be long in the land which the LORD your God gives you."

41. What is meant by the Fifth Commandment?

God requires that I always honor father and mother by loving, obeying, and serving them, and caring for them in sickness, need, and old age; likewise, that I should respect all who, in God's providence, are my superiors.

Prov. 1:8. Hear, my son, your father's instruction, and reject not your mother's teaching.

Eph. 6:1-3. Children, obey your parents in the Lord, for this is right. "Honor your father and mother" (this is the first commandment with a promise), "that it may be well with you and that you may live long on the earth."

Prov. 19:26. He who does violence to his father and chases away his mother is a son who causes shame and brings reproach.

Prov. 30:17. The eye that mocks a father and scorns to obey a mother will be picked out by the ravens of the valley and eaten by the vultures.

Heb. 13:17. Obey your leaders and submit to them; for they are keeping watch over your souls, as men who will have to give account. Let them do this joyfully, and not sadly, for that would be of no advantage to you.

Rom. 13:1. Let every person be subject to the governing authorities. For there is no authority except from God, and those that exist have been instituted by God.

Eph. 6:5-7. Slaves, be obedient to those who are your earthly masters, with fear and trembling, in singleness of heart, as to Christ; not in the way of eye-service, as men-pleasers, but as servants of Christ, doing the will of God from the heart, rendering service with a good will as to the Lord and not to men.

Acts 5:29. "We must obey God rather than men."

42. What is the Sixth Commandment?

"You shall not kill."

43. What is meant by the Sixth Commandment?

God forbids not only murder, but every deed, word, and thought, whereby my own life or the life of my fellow-man is shortened or embittered; God requires that I help my fellow-man in every need and seek his welfare for this life and the life to come.

Gen. 9:6. "Whoever sheds the blood of man, by man shall his blood be shed; for God made man in his own image."

Rom. 12:19. Beloved, never avenge yourselves, but leave it to the wrath of God; for it is written, "Vengeance is mine, I will repay, says the Lord."

Matt. 5:21, 22. "You have heard that it was said to the men of old, You shall not kill; and whoever kills shall be liable to judgment. But I say to you that every one who is angry with his brother shall be liable to judgment; whoever insults his brother shall be liable to the council, and whoever says, 'You fool!' shall be liable to the hell of fire."

1 John 3:15. Any one who hates his brother is a murderer, and you know that no murderer has eternal life abiding in him.

Matt. 5:44-45. "Love your enemies and pray for those who persecute you, so that you may be sons of your Father who is in heaven; for he makes his sun rise on the evil and on the good, and sends rain on the just and on the unjust."

Eph. 4:32. And be kind to one another, tenderhearted, forgiving one another, as God in Christ forgave you.

Isa. 1:17. "Learn to do good; seek justice, correct oppression; defend the fatherless, plead for the widow."

Matt 5:7. "Blessed are the merciful, for they shall obtain mercy."

Prov. 24:1-2. Be not envious of evil men, nor desire to be with them; for their minds devise violence, and their lips talk of mischief.

44. What is the Seventh Commandment?

"You shall not commit adultery."

45. What is meant by the Seventh Commandment?

God forbids the breaking of the marriage vow and requires all of us to be chaste in thought, word, and deed.

Matt. 5:8. "Blessed are the pure in heart, for they shall see God."

1 Cor. 6:19-20. Do you not know that your body is a temple of the Holy Spirit within you, which you have from God? You are not your own; you were bought with a price. So glorify God in your body.

Prov. 4:23. Keep your heart with all vigilance; for from it flow the springs of life.

1 Cor. 3:17. If any one destroys God's temple, God will destroy him. For God's temple is holy, and that temple you are.

Eph. 5:3-4. But immortality and all impurity or covetousness must not even be named among you, as is fitting among saints. Let there be no filthiness, nor silly talk, nor levity, which are not fitting; but instead let there be thanksgiving.

1 Cor. 15:33. "Bad company ruins good morals."

46. What is the Eighth Commandment?

"You shall not steal."

47. What is meant by the Eighth Commandment?

God forbids not only robbery and theft, but all unfair and dishonest dealings, and requires that we should help to improve and protect our neighbor's possessions and livelihood.

Hab. 2:9. Woe to him who gets evil gain for his house, to set his nest on high, to be safe from the reach of harm!

Deut. 25:13-15. "You shall not have in your bag two kinds of weights, a large and a small. You shall not have in your house two kinds of measures, a large and a small. A full and just weight you shall have, a full and just measure you shall have."

Deut. 27:17. " 'Cursed be he who removes his neighbor's landmark.' "

Ps. 37:21. The wicked borrows, and cannot pay back.

Jer. 22:13. "Woe to him who builds his house by unrighteousness, and his upper rooms by injustice; who makes his neighbor serve him for nothing."

Eph. 4:28. Let the thief no longer steal, but rather let him labor, doing honest work with his hands, so that he may be able to give to those in need.

1 Thess. 4:11-12. Aspire to live quietly, to mind your own affairs, and to work with your hands, as we charged you; so that you may command the respect of outsiders, and be dependent on nobody.

2 Cor. 9:7. God loves a cheerful giver.

48. What is the Ninth Commandment?

"You shall not bear false witness against your neighbor."

49. What is meant by the Ninth Commandment?

God forbids perjury, slander, and all manner of falsehood, and requires not only that we should be truthful and sincere in our lives, but also that we should protect the honor and good name of our fellow-man.

Prov. 19:5. A false witness will not go unpunished, and he who utters lies will not escape.

Ps. 34:13-14. Keep your tongue from evil, and your lips from speaking deceit. Depart from evil, and do good; seek pace, and pursue it.

Eph. 4:25. Therefore, putting away falsehood, let every one speak the truth with his neighbor, for we are members one of another.

Lev. 19:16. "You shall not go up and down as a slanderer among your people."

Luke 6:37. "Judge not, and you will not be judged; condemn not, and you will not be condemned; forgive, and you will be forgiven."

Isa. 5:20. Woe to those who call evil good and good evil, who put darkness for light and light for darkness, who put bitter for sweet and sweet for bitter!

Phil. 4:8. Finally, brethren, whatever is true, what-is honorable, whatever is just, whatever is pure, whatever is lovely, whatever is gracious if there is any excellence, if there is anything worthy of praise, think about these things.

50. What is the Tenth Commandment?

"You shall not covet your neighbor's house; you shall not cover your neighbor's wife, or his man-servant, or his maidservant, or his ox, or his ass, or anything that is your neighbor's."

51. What is meant by the Tenth Commandment?

God forbids all evil lusts and desires for wrongful possession or enjoyment, and requires that we seek our joy in him and in his loving care for us.

Jas. 1:14-15. But each person is tempted when he is lured and enticed by his own desire. Then desire when it has conceived gives birth to sin; and sin when it is full-grown brings forth death.

Rom. 6:12. Let not sin therefore reign in your mortal bodies, to make you obey their passions.

1 John 2:15-17. Do not love the world or the things in the world. If any one loves the world, love for the Father is not in him. For all that is in the world, the lust of the flesh and the lust of the eyes and the pride of life, is not of the Father but is of the world. And the world passes away, and the lust of it; but he who does the will of God abides for ever.

Ps. 37:4. Take delight in the LORD, and he will give you the desires of your heart.

Prov. 23:26. My son, give me your heart, and let your eyes observe my ways.

52. What is the summary of the Ten Commandments?

"You shall love the LORD your God with all your heart, and with all your soul, and with all your might." (Deut. 6:5.) "You shall love your neighbor as yourself." (Lev. 19:18.) "On these two commandments depend all the law and the prophets." (Matt. 22:40.)

53. What does God declare concerning these Commandments?

God says: " 'Cursed be he who does not confirm the words of this law by doing them.' " (Duet. 27:26; Gal. 3:10.) "You shall therefore keep my statutes and my ordinances, by doing which a man shall live: I am the LORD." (Lev. 18:5; Luke 10: 28.)

54. What is meant by this declaration?

God threatens to punish all who break his Commandments, but to those who keep them he promises grace and blessing. We should therefore fear to do wrong and seek to do God's will.

55. Have you, or has anyone, ever perfectly kept the Law of God?

No man has ever perfectly kept the Law of God. By nature we are inclined to evil and have in many ways disobeyed God's Commandments and therefore well deserve the curse of the Law.

Ps. 130:3. If thou, O LORD, shouldst mark iniquities, LORD, who could stand?

Ps. 143:2. Enter not into judgment with they servant; for no man living is righteous before thee.

Rom. 3:20. For no human being will be justified in his sight by works of the law since through the law comes knowledge of sin.

56. Can we in any way escape the curse of the Law and be saved?

We can escape the curse of the Law and be saved through the grace of God, by which the Gospel of Jesus Christ is given to us.

57. What has God in his grace and mercy done to save us?

For God so loved the world that he gave his only Son, that whoever believes in him should not perish but have eternal life. (John 3:16).

But when the time had fully come, God sent forth his Son, born of woman, born under the law, to redeem those who were under the law, so that we might receive adoption as sons. (Gal. 4:4-5.)

The Second Article of the Christian Faith

58. What is the Second Article of the Christian Faith?

I believe in Jesus Christ, his only begotten son, our Lord: who was conceived by the Holy Spirit, born of the Virgin Mary; suffered under Pontius Pilate, was crucified, dead, and buried, he descended into hell; the third day he rose again from the dead; he ascended into heaven, and sitteth at the right hand of God the Father Almighty; from thence he shall come to judge the quick and the dead.

59. Of what does the Second Article of the Christian
Faith treat?

The Second Article treats of Jesus Christ, the
Son of God, and of the work of redemption.

60. Who is Jesus Christ?

Jesus Christ is true God and true man in one
person, my Saviour, Redeemer, and Lord.

61. How does the Bible testify that Jesus Christ is
true God?

In the Bible Jesus Christ is called God; further-
more, the Bible testifies to his divine nature and
works, and demands divine honors for him.

John 1:1-3. In the beginning was the Word, and the
Word was with God, and the Word was God. He was in the
beginning with God; all things were made through him,
and without him was not anything made that was made.

John 10:30. "I and the Father are one."

John 20:28. Thomas answered him, "My Lord and
my God!"

John 17:5. And now, Father, glorify thou me in thy
own presence with the glory which I had with thee before
the world was made.

John 8:58. Jesus said to them "Truly, truly, I say to
you, before Abraham was, I am."

Matt. 11:27. "All things have been delivered to me by
my Father; and no one knows the Son except the Father,
and no one knows the Father except the Son and any one
to whom the Son chooses to reveal him."

John 5:21, 26. "For as the Father raises the dead and
gives them life, so also the Son gives life to whom he will.
For as the Father has life in himself, so he has granted
the son also to have life in himself."

Matt. 9:6. "But that you may know that the Son of man has authority on earth to forgive sins"—he then said to the paralytic—"Rise, take up your bed and go home."

John 5:22-23. "The Father judges no one, but has given all judgment to the Son, that all may honor the Son, even as they honor the Father. He who does not honor the Son does not honor the Father who sent him."

Col. 2:9. For in him the whole fullness of deity dwells bodily.

John 9:35-37.

62. How does the Bible testify that the Son of God became true man?

Jesus Christ was conceived by the Holy Spirit and born of the Virgin Mary; he thereby entered into human nature and became in all things as we are, yet without sin.

Luke 1:35. And the angel said to her, "The Holy Spirit will come upon you, and the power of the Most High will overshadow you; therefore the child to be born will be called holy, the Son of God."

John 1:14. And the Word became flesh and dwelt among us, full of grace and truth; we have beheld his glory, glory as of the only Son from the Father.

Luke 2:52. And Jesus increased in wisdom and in stature, and in favor with God and man.

Matt. 4:2. And he fasted forty days and forty nights, and afterward he was hungry.

John 19:28. After this Jesus, knowing that all was now finished, said (to fulfil the scripture), "I thirst."

John 4:6. So Jesus, wearied as he was with his journey, sat down beside the well.

Matt. 8:24. But he was asleep.

Luke 19:41. And when he drew near and saw the city he wept over it.

John 11:35. Jesus wept.

John 19:30. And he bowed his head, and gave up his spirit.

63. How did Christ reveal himself as the Saviour before his death?

Christ revealed himself as the Saviour before his death by his holy life, in which he perfectly fulfilled the Law of God; by his preaching the forgiveness of sin through faith in him; by his miracles, which are all works of life.

John 4:34. Jesus said to them, "My food is to the will of him who sent me, and to accomplish his work."

John 8:46. "Which of you convicts me of sin? If I tell the truth, why do you not believe?"

Mark 1:15. Jesus said, "The time is fulfilled, and the kingdom of God is at hand; repent, and believe in the gospel."

Luke 19:10. For the Son of man came to seek and to save the lost.

Acts 10:38. "God anointed Jesus of Nazareth with the Holy Spirit and with power; how he went about doing good and healing all that were oppressed by the devil, for God was with him."

John 5:36. "These very works which I am doing, bear me witness that the Father has sent me."

64. Whereby did Christ accomplish our redemption?

Christ accomplished our redemption by his suffering and death, in which he endured, in our

stead, the wrath of God against sin, thereby re-
deeming us from sin, satan, and death.

Isa. 53: 4. Surely he has borne our griefs and carried
our sorrows; yet we esteemed him stricken, smitten by
God, and afflicted. But he was wounded for our transgressions, he was bruised for our iniquities; upon him
was the chastisement that made us whole, and with his
stripes we are healed. All we like sheep have gone astray;
we have turned every one to his own way; and the Lord
has laid on him the iniquity of us all.

2 Cor. 5:19. God was in Christ reconciling the world
to himself, not counting their trespasses against them, and
entrusting to us the message of reconciliation.

2 Cor. 5:20. So we are ambassadors for Christ, God
making his appeal through us. We beseech you on behalf
of Christ, be reconciled to God.

2 Cor. 5:21. For our sake he made him to be sin who
knew no sin, so that in him we might become the righteousness
of God.

1 Pet. 1:18-19. You know that you were ransomed
from the futile ways inherited from your fathers, not with
perishable things such as silver or gold, but with the
precious blood of Christ, like that of a lamb without
blemish or spot.

Titus 2:14. Jesus Christ, who gave himself for us to
redeem us from all iniquity and to purify for himself a
people of his own who are zealous for good deeds.

2 Tim. 1:10. Christ Jesus, who abolished death and
brought life and immortality to light through the gospel.

Col. 1:13-14. He has delivered us from the dominion
of darkness and transfered us to the kingdom of his beloved Son, in whom we have redemption, the forgiveness
of sins.

1 John 3:16. By this we know love, that he laid down
his life for us; and we ought to lay down our lives for
the brethren.

1 John 4:10. In this is love, not that we loved God but that he loved us and sent his Son to be the expiation for our sins.

65. Why was the death of Christ necessary for our redemption?

The death of Christ was necessary for our redemption because we, lost sinners, could be redeemed neither by teaching nor by example, but only by the sacrifice of our Lord Jesus Christ in his suffering and death.

1 Cor. 2:2. For I decided to know nothing among you except Jesus Christ and him crucified.

1 Cor. 1:23-24. But we preach Christ crucified, a stumbling-block to Jews and folly to Gentiles, but to those who are called, both Jews and Greeks, Christ the power of God and the wisdom of God.

John 1:29. The next day he saw Jesus coming toward him, and said, "Behold, the Lamb of God, who takes away the sin of the world!"

Heb. 7:26-27. For it was fitting that we should have such a high priest, holy, blameless, unstained, separated from sinners, exalted above the heavens. He has no need, like those high priests, to offer sacrifices daily, first for his own sins and then for those of the people; he did this once for all when he offered up himself.

John 15:13. "Greater love has no man than this, that a man lay down his life for his friends."

66. Of what importance is Christ's burial?

Christ's burial is a testimony that he had really died.

67. What is meant when we say, "He descended into hell"?

This statement means that Jesus went to the place of departed spirits and brought them the message of salvation.

1 Pet. 3:18-20. For Christ also died for sins once for all, the righteous for the unrighteous, that he might bring us to God, being put to death in the flesh but made alive in the spirit; in which he went and preached to the spirits in prison, who formerly did not obey, when God's patience waited in the days of Noah, during the building of the ark, in which a few, that is, eight persons, were saved through water.

68. What does it mean to us that Jesus Christ arose from the dead?

The resurrection of Jesus Christ proves that he is the Son of God; that he is our Redeemer, in whom we have newness of life; and that we also shall be raised from the dead.

Rom. 4:25. Who was put to death for our trespasses and raised for our justification.

Rom. 1:4. And designated Son of God in power according to the Spirit of Holiness by his resurrection from the dead, Jesus Christ our Lord.

2. Cor. 5:15. And he died for all, that those who live might live no longer for themselves but for him who for their sake died and was raised.

1 Cor. 15:17-18. If Christ has not been raised, your faith is futile and you are still in your sins. Then those also who have fallen asleep in Christ have perished.

1 Cor. 15:20-21. But in fact Christ has been raised from the dead, the first fruits of those who have fallen asleep. For as by a man came death, by a man has come also the resurrection of the dead.

Rom. 8:11. If the Spirit of him who raised Jesus from the dead dwells in you, he who raised Christ Jesus from the dead will give life to your mortal bodies also through his Spirit which dwells in you.

Rom. 6:4. So that as Christ was raised from the dead by the glory of the Father, we too might walk in newness of life.

John 11:25-26. Jesus said to her, "I am the resurrection and the life; he who believes in me, though he die, yet shall he live, and whoever lives and believes in me shall never die."

69. What does it mean to us that Christ ascended into heaven?

Forty days after his resurrection, Christ was visibly taken up into heaven, there to prepare a place for us.

John 14:2-3. "In my Father's house are many rooms; if it were not so, would I have told you that I go to prepare a place for you? And when I go and prepare a place for you, I will come again and will take you to myself, that where I am you may be also."

John 17:24. "Father, I desire that they also, whom thou hast given me, may be with me where I am, to behold my glory which thou hast given me in thy love for me."

Read Acts 1:1-11.

70. What do we confess by the words "He sitteth at the right hand of God the Father Almighty"?

By these words we confess that the risen and ascended Christ is is heaven in the full power and glory of God.

Ps. 110:1. The LORD says to my lord: "Sit at my right hand, till I make your enemies your footstool."

Eph. 1:20-23. Which he accomplished in Christ when he raised him from the dead and made him sit at his right hand in the heavenly places, far above all rule and authority and power and dominion, and above every name that is named, not only in this age but also in that which is to come; and he has put all things under his feet and has made him the head over all things for the church, which is his body, the fullness of him who fills all in all.

Rom. 8:33-34. Who shall bring any charge against God's elect? It is God who justifies; who is to condemn? Is it Christ Jesus, who died, yes who was raised from the dead, who is at the right hand of God, who indeed intercedes for us?

71. What do we confess with the words "From thence he shall come to judge the quick and the dead"?

With these words we confess that Christ will come again on the last day with great power and glory to take into eternal life those who believe, and to deliver into eternal death those who do not believe.

Acts 1:11. "This Jesus, who was taken up from you into heaven, will come in the same way as you saw him go into heaven."

Luke 21:27-28. "And then they will see the Son of man coming in a cloud with power and great glory. Now when these things begin to take place, look up and raise your heads, because your redemption is drawing near."

Matt. 25:31-32. "When the Son of man comes in his glory, and all the angels with him, then he will sit on his glorious throne. Before him will be gathered all the nations, and he will separate them one from another as a shepherd separates the sheep from the goats."

2 Cor. 5:10. For we must all appear before the judgment seat of Christ, so that each one may receive good or evil, according to what he has done in the body.

72. In which passage of Holy Scripture do we find the humiliation and the exaltation of Christ briefly described?

We find the humiliation and the exaltation of Christ briefly described in the passage Philippians 2:5-11: Have this mind among yourselves, which you have in Christ Jesus, who, though he was in the form of God, did not count equality with God a thing to be grasped, but emptied himself, taking the form of a servant, being born in the likeness of men. And being found in human form he humbled himself and became obedient unto death, even death on a cross. Therefore God has highly exalted him and bestowed on him the name which is above every name, that at the name of Jesus every knee should bow, in heaven and on earth and under the earth, and every tongue confess that Jesus Christ is Lord, to the glory of God the Father.

73. A Summary of the Second Article of the Christian Faith.

1. Who is Jesus Christ?

I believe that Jesus Christ—true God, begotten of the Father from eternity, and also true man, born of the Virgin Mary—is my Lord.

2. What did Christ do for you?

He has redeemed, purchased, and delivered me, a lost and condemned creature, from all sins, from death and from the power of satan.

3. How did he redeem you?

Not with silver or gold, but with his holy, precious blood, and with his innocent suffering and death.

4. To what purpose did he redeem you?

That I might be his own, live under him in his
kingdom, and serve him in everlasting righteousness, innocence, and blessedness, even as he is
risen from the dead, lives and reigns in all eternity.

The Third Article of the Christian Faith

74. What is the Third Article of the Christian Faith?

I believe in the Holy Spirit; the one holy universal Christian Church; the communion of
saints; the forgiveness of sins; the resurrection
of the body; and the life everlasting. Amen.

75. Of what does the Third Article of the Christian
Faith treat?

The Third Article of the Christian Faith treats
of God the Holy Spirit and of the godly life which
he makes possible.

76. What do we believe about the Holy Spirit?

We believe that the Holy Spirit is the third
person in the Holy Trinity, with the Father and
the Son, true and eternal God, a Lord and dis-
tributor of all gifts, who enables us to come to
Christ, our Lord, and to remain with him forever.

77. By what means does the Holy Spirit do his work?

The Holy Spirit works through the Word of
God and the Holy Sacraments, which are the
means of grace.

Jas. 1:21. Therefore put away all filthiness and rank growth of wickedness and receive with meekness the implanted word, which is able to save your souls.

Acts 2:38. "Repent and be baptized every one of you in the name of Jesus Christ for the forgiveness of your sins; and you shall receive the gift of the Holy Spirit."

1 Cor. 10:16. The cup of blessing which we bless, is it not a participation in the blood of Christ? The bread which we break, is it not a participation in the body of Christ?

78. In what manner does the Holy Spirit lead us to Christ?

The Holy Spirit makes known to us the call of God to come to Christ; he teaches us how, because of our sin, we need Christ; he leads us by repentance and faith to accept and follow Christ; he enables us to thus to begin and live the new life of a child of God.

Heb. 3:7-8. Therefore, as the Holy Spirit says, "To-day, when you hear his voice, do not harden your hearts."

John 15:26. "But when the Counselor comes, whom I shall send to you from the Father, even the Spirit of truth, who proceeds from the Father, he will bear witness to me."

John 14:26. "But the Counselor, the Holy Spirit, whom the Father will send in my name, he will teach you all things, and bring to your remembrance all that I have said to you."

Rom. 8:9, 14. Any one who does not have the Spirit of Christ does not belong to him. For all who are led by the Spirit of God are sons of God.

John 16:13. "When the Spirit of truth comes, he will guide you into all the truth."

79. What is repentance?

True repentance consists in conviction of sin, sorrow for sin, confession and renunciation of sin, and longing for grace.

Ps. 38:4. For my iniquities have gone over my head; they weigh like a burden too heavy for me.

2 Cor. 7:10. For godly grief produces a repentance that leads to salvation and brings no regret, but worldly grief produces death.

Matt. 5:4. "Blessed are those who mourn, for they shall be comforted."

Ps. 51:17. The sacrifice acceptable to God is a broken spirit; a broken and contrite heart, O God, thou wilt not despise.

1 John 1:8-9. If we say we have no sin, we deceive ourselves, and the truth is not in us. If we confess our sins, he is faithful and just, and will forgive our sins and cleanse us from all unrighteousness.

Jas. 5:16. Therefore confess your sins to one another.

Prov. 28:13. He who conceals his transgressions will not prosper, but he who confesses and forsakes them will obtain mercy.

Isa. 55:7. "Let the wicked forsake his way, and the unrighteous man his thoughts; let him return to the LORD, that he may have mercy on him, and to our God, for he will abundantly pardon."

Luke 19:8. And Zacchaeus stood and said to the Lord, "Behold, Lord, the half of my goods I give to the poor; and if I have defrauded any one of anything, I restore it fourfold."

Luke 15:18-19. I will arise and go to my father, and I will say to him, "Father, I have sinned against heaven and before you; I am no longer worthy to be called your son; treat me as one of your hired servants."

Luke 18:13. " 'God, be merciful to me a sinner!' "

Matt. 5:6. "Blessed are those who hunger and thirst for righteousness, for they shall be satisfied."

80. What is faith?

Faith is complete trust in God and willing acceptance of his grace in Jesus Christ.

Heb. 11:1. Now faith is the assurance of things hoped for, the conviction of things not seen.

Heb. 11:6. And without faith it is impossible to please him. For whoever would draw near to God must believe that he exists and that he rewards those who seek him.

1 Tim. 1:15. The saying is sure and worthy of full acceptance, that Christ Jesus came into the world to save sinners. And I am the foremost of the sinners.

John 6:40. "For this is the will of my Father, that every one who sees the Son and believe in him should have eternal life."

John 6:68-69. "Lord, to whom shall we go? You have the words of eternal life; and we have believed, and have come to know, that you are the Holy One of God."

Acts 16:31. And they said, "Believe in the Lord Jesus, and you will be saved, you and you household."

81. What does God do for us when we come to him in in repentance and faith?

When we come to God in repentance and faith, he forgives us our sins for Jesus' sake, counts the merit of Christ as belonging to us, and accepts us as his children. This is justification.

1 John 3:1. See what love the Father has given us, that we should be called children of God; and so we are. The reason why the world does not know us is that it did not know him.

Gal. 3:26. For in Christ Jesus you are all sons of God, through faith.

Rom. 3:23-24. All have sinned and fall short of the glory of God, they are justified by his grace as a gift, through the redemption which is in Christ Jesus.

Rom. 3:28. For we hold that a man is justified by faith apart from works of law.

Eph. 2:8-9. For by grace you have been saved through faith; and this is not you own doing, it is the gift of God —not because of works, lest any man should boast.

82. How does the Bible speak of the change in our life brought about by repentance and faith?

The Bible speaks of this change as being born again, or as being converted.

83. What does it mean to be born again?

To be born again means the beginning of the new life within us by the power of God's word and the sacrament of baptism. This is regeneration.

John 3:3. Jesus answered him, "Truly, truly, I say to you, unless one is born anew, he cannot see the kingdom of God."

John 3:5. Jesus answered, "Truly, truly, I say to you, unless one is born of water and the Spirit, he cannot enter the kingdom of God."

Gal. 3:27. For as many of you as were baptized into Christ have put on Christ.

1 Pet. 1:23. You have been born anew, not of perishable seed but of imperishable, through the living and abiding word of God.

84. What does it mean to be converted?

To be converted means to turn from the broad way of the sinful life and to enter the narrow way of the godly life. (This is conversion.)

Matt. 7:13-14. "Enter by the narrow gate; for the gate is wide and the way is easy, that leads to destruction, and those who enter by it are many. For the gate is narrow and the way is hard, that leads to life, and those who find it are few."

Ezek. 33:11. "As I live, says the Lord God, I have no pleasure in the death of the wicked, but that the wicked turn from his way and live; turn back, turn back from your evil ways."

Ezek. 18:21. "But if a wicked man turns away from all his sins which he has committed and keeps all my statutes and does what is lawful and right, he shall surely live; he shall not die."

1 Pet. 2:25. For you were straying like sheep, but have now returned to the Shepherd and Guardian of your souls.

85. Whereby are we assured of our justification?

We are assured of our justification by the testimony of the Holy Spirit, as it is written Romans 8:15-16: For you did not receive the spirit of slavery to fall back into fear, but you have received the spirit of sonship. When we cry, "Abba! Father!" It is the Spirit himself bearing witness with our spirit that we are children of God.

86. What is necessary for us to continue in the godly life?

In order that we may continue in the godly life the Holy Spirit must daily transform and renew us in all our thoughts and actions and make us acceptable to God. This is sancitification.

1 John 5:4. For whatever is born of God overcomes the world; and this is the victory that overcomes the world, our faith.

2 Cor. 5:17. Therefore, if any one is in Christ, he is a new creation; the old has passed away, behold, the new has come.

2 Pet. 3:18. But grow in the grace and knowledge of our Lord and Savior Jesus Christ.

1 Pet. 2:1-2.

Eph. 4:22-24. Put off your old nature which belongs to your former manner of life and is corrupt through deceitful lusts, and be renewed in the spirit of your minds, and put on the new nature, created after the likeness of God in true righteousness and holiness.

Phil. 3:12. Not that I have already obtained this or am already perfect; but I press on to make it my own, because Christ Jesus has made me his own.

Heb. 12:14. Strive for peace with all men, and for the holiness without which no one will see the Lord.

1 Thess. 5:23. May the God of peace himself sanctify you wholly; and may your spirit and soul and body be kept sound and blameless at the coming of our Lord Jesus Christ.

87. What is meant by "Church" in the Apostles' Creed?
By the one holy universal Christian Church we mean the entire body of true Christians.

John 17:20-21. "I do not pray for these only, but also for those who are to believe in me through their word, that they may all be one."

88. Why is the Church called "one" Church?

The Christian Church is called the "one" Church because it has one Lord, one faith, one baptism, one God and Father of all, as it is written Ephesians 4:3-6: Eager to maintain the unity of the Spirit in the bond of peace. There is one body and one Spirit, just as you were called to the one hope that belongs to your call, one Lord, one faith, one baptism, one God and Father of us all, who is above all and through all and in all.

89. Why is the Church called holy?

The church is called holy because the Holy Spirit works mightily in it by Word and Sacrament to the end that all its members shall be made holy.

Eph. 5:25-27. Christ loved the church and gave himself up for her, that he might sanctify her, having cleansed her by the washing of water with the word, that the church might be presented before him in splendor, without spot or wrinkle or any such thing, that she might be holy and without blemish.

1 Pet. 2:9. But you are a chosen race, a royal priesthood, a holy nation, God's own people, that you may declare the wonderful deeds of him who called you out of darkness into his marvelous light.

90. What is the Church called universal?

The Church is called universal because god has meant it for all men, and because everyone finds in it what he needs.

John 10:16. "And I have other sheep, that are not of this fold; I must bring them also, and they will heed my voice. So there shall be one flock, one shepherd."

Mark 16:15. *"Go into all the world, and preach the gospel to the whole creation."*

91. Why is the Church called the "Christian" Church?

The Church is called Christian because Christ alone in its foundation, its head, and its ideal.

1. Cor. 3:11. For no other foundation can anyone lay than that which is laid, which is Jesus Christ.

Col. 1:18. He is the head of the body, the church.

Eph. 4:13. Until we all attain to the unity of the faith and of the knowledge of the Son of God, to mature manhood, to the measure of the stature of the fullness of Christ.

Eph. 4:15. We are to grow up in every way into him who is the head, into Christ.

92. What is the mission of the Church?

The mission of the Church is to extend the Kingdom of God, that is, to lead men to Christ and to establish Christian principles in every relation of life.

Acts 1:8. "You shall be my witnesses in Jerusalem and in all Judea and Samaria and to the end of the earth."

Isa. 52:7. How beautiful upon the mountains are the feet of him who brings good tidings, who publishes peace, who brings good tidings of good, who publishes salvation, who says to Zion, "Your God reigns."

Rom. 10:14. But how are men to call upon him in whom they have not believed? And how are they to believe in him of whom they have never heard? And how are they to hear without a preacher?

Luke 9:2. And he sent them out to preach the kingdom of God and to heal.

Matt. 24:14. "And this gospel of the kingdom will be preached throughout the whole world, as a testimony to all nations."

Luke 13:19. "The kingdom of God is like a grain of mustard seed which a man took and sowed in his garden; and it grew and became a tree, and the birds of the air made nests in its branches."

Matt. 13:33. "The kingdom of heaven is like leaven which a woman took and hid in three measures of meal, till it was all leavened."

93. What is the Kingdom of God?

The Kingdom of God is the rule of God established in the hearts and lives of men.

Luke 17:20-21. Being asked by the Pharisees when the kingdom of God was coming, he answered them, "The kingdom of God is not coming with signs to be observed; nor will they say, 'Lo, here it is!' or 'There!' for behold, the kingdom of God is in the midst of you."

John 18:36. Jesus answered, "My kingship is not of this world; if my kingship were of this world, my servants would fight, that I might not be handed over to the Jews; but my kingship is not from the world."

Luke 6:31. "And as you wish that men would do to you, do so to them."

Luke 6:44-45. "For each tree is known by its own fruit. For figs are not gathered from thorns, nor are grapes picked from a bramble bush. The good man out of the good treasure of his heart produces good, and the evil man out of his evil treasure produces evil; for out of the abundance of the heart his mouth speaks."

Matt. 5:16. "Let your light so shine before men, that they may see your good works and give glory to your Father who is in heaven."

Matt. 5:44-45. "But I say to you, Love your enemies and pray for those who persecute you, that you may be sons of your Father who is in heaven; for he makes his sun rise on the evil and on the good, and sends rain on the just and on the unjust."

94. Where did Christ set forth the principles of his Kingdom?

Christ set forth the principles of his Kingdom in the Sermon on the Mount. (Matthew, chapters 5-7. Luke, chapter 6, verses 20-49.)

95. Has the Church already become all that we confess concerning it?

The Church has indeed existed at all times as the true Church, but has frequently erred and been corrupted; its future perfection, however, is certain, according to God's promise.

Matt. 16:18. "And I tell you, you are Peter, and on this rock I will build my church, and the powers of death shall not prevail against it."

Matt. 13:24-26. "The kingdom of heaven may be compared to a man who sowed good seed in his field; but while men were sleeping, his enemy came and sowed weeds among the wheat, and went away. So when the plants came up and bore grain, then the weeds appeared also."

96. What do we understand by the communion of saints?

By the communion of saints we understand that all Christians, as members of one body, should love and help one another in all things.

1 Cor. 12:12-13. For just as the body is one and has many members, and all the members of the body, though many, are one body, so it is with Christ. For by one Spirit we were all baptized into one body.

Phil 2:2-4. Complete my joy by being of the same mind, having the same love, being in full accord and of one mind. Do nothing from selfishness or conceit, but in humility count others better than yourselves. Let each of you look not only to his own interests, but also to the interests of others.

1 Cor. 12:26. If one member suffers, all suffer together; if one member is honored, all rejoice together.

97. What do we mean by the words "I believe in the forgiveness of sins"?

The forgiveness of sins is present in Christ for all mankind, and is offered by the grace of God to all sinners.

Luke 24:46-47. "Thus it is written, that the Christ should suffer and on the third day rise from the dead, and that repentance and forgiveness of sins should be preached in his name to all nations."

Mark 3:28. "Truly, I say to you, all sins will be forgiven the sons of men."

1 John 2:1-2. If any one does sin, we have an advocate with the Father, Jesus Christ the righteous; and he is the expiation for our sins, and not for ours only but also for the sins of the whole world.

Isa. 1:18. "Though your sins are like scarlet, they shall be as white as snow; though, they are red like crimson, they shall become like wool."

98. What do we understand by the resurrection of the body?

On the last day Christ will raise up all the dead, as it is written (John 5:28-29): "Do not marvel at this, for the hour is coming when all who are in the tombs will hear his voice and come forth, those who have done good, to the resurrection of life, and those who have done evil, to the resurrection of judgment."

1 Cor. 15:42-44. What is sown is perishable, what is raised is imperishable. It is sown in dishonor, it is raised in glory. It is sown in weakness, it is raised in power. It is sown a physical body, it is raised a spiritual body.

Phi. 3:20-21. But our commonwealth is in heaven, and from it we await a Savior, the Lord Jesus Christ, who will change our lowly body to be like his glorious body, by the power which enables him even to subject all things to himself.

John 17:24. "Father, I desire that they also, whom thou hast given me, may be with me where I am, to behold my glory which thou hast given me."

2 Cor. 5:10. For we must all appear before the judgment seat of Christ so that each one may receive good or evil, according to what he has done in the body.

99. What do we mean by the life everlasting?

By the life everlasting we mean that in the resurrection all children of God shall receive the glory of Christ in body and soul and shall abide with him forever.

1 John 3:2. Beloved, we are God's children now; it does not yet appear what we shall be, but we know that when he appears we shall be like him, for we shall see him as he is.

1 Cor. 13:12. For now we see in a mirror dimly, but then face to face. Now I know in part; then I shall understand fully, even as I have been fully understood.

Matt. 25:34. "Come, O blessed of my Father, inherit the kingdom prepared for you from the foundation of the world."

Isa. 35:10. And the ransomed of the LORD shall return, and come to Zion with singing, with everlasting joy upon their heads; they shall obtain joy and gladness, and sorrow and sighing shall flee away.

Rev. 21:3-4. "Behold, the dwelling of God is with men. He will dwell with them, and they shall be his people, and God himself will be with them; he will wipe away every tear from their eyes, and death shall be no more, neither shall there be mourning nor crying nor pain any more, for the former things have passed away."

100. A summary of the Third Article of the Christian Faith.

1. How do you become a true Christian?

I believe that I can not by my own reason or strength believe in my Lord Jesus Christ, or come to him; but the Holy Spirit has called me by the Gospel, enlightened me with his gifts, sanctified and preserved me in the true faith.

2. Through what institution does the Holy Spirit work?

The Holy Spirit calls, gathers, enlightens, and preserves the whole Christian Church on earth and keeps it with Jesus Christ in the one true faith.

3. What do you receive in the Church through the Holy Spirit?

In the Christian Church the Holy Spirit daily and abundantly forgives me and all believers all sins.

4. What is your hope for the future?

On the last day Christ will raise up me and all the dead and will give to me and all believers everlasting life. This is most certainly true.

PART III
PRAYER

101. What is prayer?

Prayer is the conversation of the heart with God for the purpose of praising him, asking him to supply the needs of ourselves and others, and thanking him for whatever he gives us.

Ps. 19:14. Let the words of my mouth and the meditation of my heart be acceptable in thy sight, O LORD, my rock and my redeemer.

Ps. 34:3. O magnify the LORD with me, and let us exalt his name together!

Ps. 103:1-4. Bless the LORD, O my soul; and all that is within me, bless his holy name! Bless the LORD, O my soul, and forget not all his benefits, who forgives all your iniquity, who heals all your diseases, who redeems your life from the Pit, who crowns you with steadfast love and mercy.

Matt. 6:6. "But when you pray, go into your room and shut the door and pray to your Father who is in secret; and your Father who sees in secret will reward you."

Matt. 7:7-8. "Ask, and it will be given you; seek and you will find; knock, and it will be opened to you. For every one who asks receives, and he who seeks finds, and to him who knocks it will be opened."

Matt. 18:19-20. "Again I say to you, if two of you agree on earth about anything they ask, it will be done for them by my Father in heaven. For where two or three are gathered in my name, there am I in the midst of them."

Matt. 21:22. "And whatever you ask in prayer, you will receive, if you have faith."

Eph. 5:20. Always and for everything giving thanks in the name of our Lord Jesus Christ to God the Father.

Ps. 92:1. It is good to give thanks to the LORD, to sing praises to thy name, O Most High.

1 Tim. 2:1-2. First of all, then, I urge that supplications, prayers, intercessions, and thanksgivings be made for all men, for kings and all who are in high positions, that we may lead a quiet and peaceable life, godly and respectful in every way.

1 Thess. 5:17. Pray constantly.

102. In what prayer has the Lord Jesus taught us how to pray?

Jesus taught us to pray in the Lord's Prayer: "Our Father who art in heaven, Hallowed be thy name. Thy kingdom come, Thy will be done, On earth as it is in heaven. Give us this day our daily bread; And forgive us our debts, As we also have forgiven our debtors; And lead us not into temptation, But deliver us from evil." *For thine is the kingdom, and the power, and the glory, forever. Amen.*   (Matthew 6:9-13; Luke 11:1-4.)

103. What is the meaning of "Our Father who art in heaven"?

Our heavenly Father desires us and all his children to call upon him with cheerful confidence, as beloved children entreat a kind and affectionate father, knowing that he is both willing and able to help us.

Matt. 7:9-11. "Or what man of you, if his son asks him for a loaf, will give him a stone? Or if he asks for a fish, will give him a serpent? If you then, who are evil, know how to give good gifts to your children, how much more will your Father who is in heaven give good things to those who ask him?"

John 16:27. "For the Father himself loves you, because you have loved me and have believed that I came from the Father."

Rom. 10:12. The same Lord is Lord of all and bestows his riches upon all who call upon him.

Ps. 121:1-2. I lift up my eyes to the hills. From whence does my help come? My help comes from the LORD, who made heaven and earth.

104. What do we pray for in the first petition: "Hallowed be thy name"?

We pray in this petition that God's name may be kept holy among us as it is holy in itself. This is done when the Word of God is taught in its truth and purity, and we as the children of God lead a holy life in accordance with it.

Ps. 72:18-19. Blessed be the LORD, the God of Israel, who alone does wondrous things. Blessed be his glorious name for ever; may his glory fill the whole earth!

Matt. 5:16. "Let your light so shine before men, that they may see your good works and give glory to your Father who is in heaven."

105. What do we pray for in the second petition: "Thy kingdom come"?

In the second petition we pray that we and all others may share in the Kingdom of God which was established by the redemption through Jesus Christ, and that its rule may be extended over all the world.

Luke 17:20-21. Being asked by the Pharisees when the kingdom of God was coming, he answered them, "The kingdom of God is not coming with signs to be observed; nor will they say, 'Lo, here it is!' or 'There!' for behold, the kingdom of God is in the midst of you."

Rev. 11:15. "The kingdom of the world has become the kingdom of our Lord and of his Christ, and he shall reign for ever and ever."

Compare Matt. 13:44—The parable of the mustard seed, and

Matt. 13:45—The parable of the leaven.

106. What do we pray for in the third petition: "Thy will be done, on earth as it is in heaven"?

In the third petition we pray that God's good and gracious will may be done by us and all men as cheerfully as it is done by the angels in heaven.

1 John 2:17. And the world passes away, and the lust of it; but he who does the will of God abides for ever.

Rom. 12:2. Do not be conformed to this world but be transformed by the renewal of your mind, that you may prove what is the will of God, what is good and acceptable and perfect.

Heb. 13:20-21. The God of peace . . . equip you with everything good that you may do his will, working in you that which is pleasing in his sight, through Jesus Christ; to whom be glory for ever and ever.

107. What do we pray for in the fourth petition: "Give us this day our daily bread"?

In the fourth petition we look to God as the One who supplies the needs of our body as well as of our soul, and we ask him to make us truly thankful for these his gifts.

Matt. 5:45. "For he makes his sun rise on the evil and on the good, and sends rain on the just and on the unjust."

Ps. 145:15-16. The eyes of all look to thee, and thou givest them their food in due season. Thou openest thy hand, thou satisfiest the desire of every living thing.

Prov. 30:8-9. Give me neither poverty nor riches; feed me with the food that is needful for me, lest I be full, and deny thee, and say, "Who is the LORD?" or lest I be poor, and steal, and profane the name of my God.

Matt. 6:34. "Therefore do not be anxious about tomorrow, for tomorrow will be anxious for itself. Let the day's own trouble be sufficient for the day."

Ps. 127:1-2. Unless the LORD builds the house, those who build it labor in vain. Unless the LORD watches over the city, the watchman stays awake in vain. It is in vain that you rise up early, to go late to rest, eating the bread of anxious toil; for he gives to his beloved in sleep.

2 Thess. 3:10. For even when we were with you, we gave you this command: If any one will not work, let him not eat.

Deut. 8:10. "And you shall eat and be full, and you shall bless the LORD your God for the good land he has given you."

Matt. 4:4. "Man shall not live by bread alone, but by every word that proceeds from the mouth of God."

108. What do we pray for in the fifth petition: "Forgive us our debts, as we also have forgiven our debtors"?

In the fifth petition we ask God for gracious forgiveness of our sins, and for willingness and strength to forgive others.

Ps. 51:1-3. Have mercy on me, O God, according to thy steadfast love; according to thy abundant mercy blot out my transgressions. Wash me thoroughly from my iniquity, and cleanse me from my sin! For I know my transgressions, and my sin is ever before me.

Matt. 6:14-15. "For if you forgive men their trespasses, your heavenly Father also will forgive you; but if you do not forgive men their trespasses, neither will your Father forgive your trespasses."

Matt. 18:21-22. Then Peter came up and said to him, "Lord, how often shall my brother sin against me, and I forgive him? As many as seven times?" Jesus said to him, "I do not say to you seven times, but seventy times seven."

109. What do we pray for in the sixth petition: "Lead us not into temptation"?

In the sixth petition we pray that whenever we are tempted by satan, the world, and our flesh to do evil, God may protect and keep us from sinning.

Jas. 1:13. Let no one say when he is tempted, "I am tempted by God"; for God cannot be tempted with evil and he himself tempts no one.

1 Cor. 10:13. God is faithful, and he will not let you be tempted beyond your strength, but with the temptation will also provide the way of escape, that you may be able to endure it.

1 Pet. 2:11. Beloved, I beseech you as aliens and exiles to abstain from the passions of the flesh that wage war against your soul.

1 John 5:4-5. This is the victory that overcomes the world, our faith. Who is it that overcomes the world but he who believes that Jesus is the Son of God?

110. What do we pray for in the seventh petition: "But deliver us from evil"?

In the seventh petition we pray that the heavenly Father may deliver us from every evil of body and soul; and finally, when our last hour has come, graciously take us from this world of sorrow to himself in heaven.

John 17:15. "I do not pray that thou shouldst take them out of the world, but that thou shouldst keep them from the evil one."

2 Tim. 4:18. The Lord will rescue me from every evil and save me for his heavenly kingdom.

Rom. 8:23. We ourselves, who have the first fruits of the Spirit, groan inwardly as we wait for adoption as sons, the redemption of our bodies.

111. What is the meaning of the closing words: For thine is the kingdom, and the power, and the glory forever?

By these closing words we mean to express our confidence that God will hear and answer our petitions; for he himself has commanded us thus to pray and promised that we shall be heard. Amen: That is, Yea, yea, it shall be so.

2 Cor. 1:20. For all the promises of God find their Yes in him. That is why we utter the Amen through him, to the glory of God.

Eph. 3:20. Now to him who by the power at work within us is able to do far more abundantly than all that we ask or think, to him be glory in the church and in Christ Jesus to all generations, for ever and ever. Amen.

112. Why is prayer necessary?

Prayer is necessary because God will give his grace and his Holy Spirit only to those who earnestly and without ceasing ask them of him and render thanks unto him.

Luke 18:7-8. "And will not God vindicate his elect, who cry to him day and night? Will he delay long over them? I tell you, he will vindicate them speedily."

Luke 11:13. "If you then, who are evil, know how to give good gifts to your children, how much more will the heavenly Father give the Holy Spirit to those who ask him?"

Ps. 55:16-17. But I call upon God; and the LORD will save me. Evening and morning and at noon I utter my complaint and moan, and he will hear my voice.

Jas. 5:16. Pray for one another, that you may be healed. The prayer of a righteous man has great power in its effects.

113. How should we pray?

We should pray humbly because of our need and unworthiness; and yet with faith, believing that for the sake of Jesus Christ, our Lord, God will certainly hear our prayer.

Dan. 9:18. "We do not present our supplications before thee on the ground of our righteousness, but on the ground of thy great mercy."

Matt. 21:22. "And whatever you ask in prayer, you will receive, if you have faith."

John 15:7. "If you abide in me, and my words abide in you, ask whatever you will, and it shall be done for you."

Jas. 1:6. But let him ask in faith, with no doubting, for he who doubts is like a wave of the sea that is driven and tossed by the wind.

114. Are all our prayers answered?

All prayers are answered either in the way we expect God to answer them or in the way God knows will be best for us.

2 Cor. 12:8-9. Three times I besought the Lord about this, that it should leave me; but he said to me, "My grace is sufficient for you, for my power is made perfect in weakness."

Ps. 40:1. I waited patiently for the Lord; he inclined to me and heard my cry.

Hab. 1:2. O Lord, how long shall I cry for help, and thou wilt not hear? Or cry to thee "Violence!" and thou wilt not save?

Gen. 32:26. But Jacob said, "I will not let you go, unless you bless me."

Ps. 10:17. O Lord, thou wilt hear the desire of the meek; thou wilt strengthen their heart, thou wilt incline thy ear.

Matt. 26:39. He fell on his face and prayed, "My Father, if it be possible, let this cup pass from me; nevertheless, not as I will, but as thou wilt."

PART IV

THE SACRAMENT OF HOLY BAPTISM

115. What is a sacrament?

A sacrament is a holy ordinance of the Church instituted by Christ himself in which by visible signs and means he imparts and preserves the new life.

116. How many sacraments has Christ instituted?

Christ has instituted two sacraments, Holy Baptism and the Lord's Supper.

117. With what words did Christ institute the sacrament of Holy Baptism?

Christ instituted the sacrament of Holy Baptism with these words in Matthew 28:18-20:

"All authority in heaven and on earth has been given to me. Go therefore and make disciples of all nations, baptizing them in the name of the Father and of the Son and of the Holy Spirit, teaching them to observe all that I have commanded you; and lo, I am with you always to the close of the age."

118. What does God do for us in Holy Baptism?

In Holy Baptism God imparts the gift of the new life unto man, receives him into his fellowship as his child, and admits him as a member of the Christian Church.

119. What does Holy Baptism require of us?

Holy Baptism requires of us that we by daily repentance renounce all sinful longings and desires, and by faith arise to a new life.

Rom. 6:3-4. Do you not know that all of us who have been baptized into Christ Jesus were baptized into his death? We were buried therefore with him by baptism into death, so that as Christ was raised from the dead by the glory of the Father, we too might walk in newness of life.

Col. 3:9-10. Seeing that you have put off the old nature with its practices and have put on the new nature, which is being renewed in knowledge after the image of its creator.

120. Why should little children be baptized?

Little children should be baptized because the new life is a gift of God's love, which little children need as much and are as able to receive as adults, for the Lord Jesus has promised unto them his Kingdom.

Acts 2:39. "For the promise is to you and to your children."

Mark 10:13, 14, 16. And they were bringing children to him, that he might touch them; and the disciples rebuked them. But when Jesus saw it he was indignant, and said to them, "Let the children come to me, do not hinder them; for to such belongs the kingdom of God." And he took them in his arms and blessed them, laying his hands upon them.

121. What does the baptism of children require of the parents?

The baptism of children requires of the parents that they help their children to grow in godly life by Christian teaching and training, by prayer and example.

Matt. 28:20. "Teaching them to observe all that I have commanded you."

Eph. 6:4. Fathers, do not provoke your children to anger, but bring them up in the discipline and instruction of the Lord.

12. What is the confirmation?

Confirmation is the renewal of the baptismal covenant. The baptized children, having been instructed in the Christian faith, publicly confess their faith in their Saviour Jesus Christ, promise obedience to him until death, and are received by the Church into active membership.

PART V

THE SACRAMENT OF THE LORD'S SUPPER

123. With what words did Christ institute the sacrament of the Lord's Supper or Holy Communion?

The Lord Jesus on the night when he was betrayed took bread, and when he had given thanks, he broke it, and gave it to the disciples and said, "Take, eat; this is my body, which is for you. Do this in remembrance of me."

In the same way also he took a cup, after supper, and when he had given thanks he gave it to them, saying, "Drink of it, all of you; for this is my blood of the covenant, which is poured out for many for the forgiveness of sins. Do this, as often as you drink it, in remembrance of me." Matt. 26: 26-28; Mark 14:22-24; Luke 22:19-20; 1 Cor. 11: 23-25.)

124. What are the visible signs and means of the sacrament of the Lord's Supper?

The visible signs and means of the sacrament of the Lord's Supper are bread and wine, partaken of by the communicant.

125. What is the Lord's Supper?

The Lord's Supper is the sacrament by which we receive the body and blood of our Lord Jesus Christ as the nourishment of our new life, strengthen the fellowship with Christ and all believers, and confess that he has died for us.

126. What blessings do we receive as we eat and drink
in the Lord's Supper?

As we eat and drink in the Lord's Supper we
receive forgiveness of sins, life and salvation. For
so it is written: Broken and shed for you for the
remission of sins.

John 6:51. "I am the living bread which came down
from heaven; if any one eats of this bread, he will live for
ever; and the bread which I shall give for the life of the
world is my flesh."

John 6:55-56. "For my flesh is food indeed, and my
blood is drink indeed. He who eats my flesh and drinks my
blood abides in me, and I in him."

Eph. 5:30. We are members of his body.

1 Cor. 10:17. Because there is one loaf, we who are
many are one body, for we all partake of the same loaf.

1 Cor. 11:26. For as often as you eat this bread and
drink the cup, you proclaim the Lord's death until he
comes.

127. On what condition do we receive the blessings of
the Lord's Supper?

We receive the blessings of the Lord's Supper
only as we eat and drink with heartfelt repentance and true faith in our Lord Jesus Christ.

1 Cor. 11:28. Let a man examine himself, and so eat
of the bread and drink of the cup.

2 Cor. 13:5. Examine yourselves, to see whether you
are holding to your faith. Test yourselves.

Ps. 139:23-24. Search me, O God, and know my heart!
Try me and know my thoughts! And see if there be any
wicked way in me, and lead me in the way everlasting!

1 Cor. 11:27. Whoever, therefore, eats the bread or drinks the cup of the Lord in an unworthy manner will be guilty of profaning the body and the blood of the Lord.

1 Cor. 11:29-30. For any one who eats and drinks without discerning the body eats and drinks judgment upon himself. That is why many of you are weak and ill, and some have died.

Matt. 5:23-24. "So if you are offering your gift at the altar, and there remember that your brother has something against you, give your gift there before the altar and go; first be reconciled to your brother, and then come and offer your gift."

128. What does our communion daily require of us?

Our communion requires that we daily keep in remembrance the crucifixion of our Lord Jesus, and that we consider well how hard it was for our Saviour to bear our sins and the sins of the whole world, and to gain eternal salvation for us by offering up his life and shedding his blood. And since our sins caused the Lord Jesus the greatest sufferings, yea bitter death, we should have no pleasure in sin, but earnestly flee and avoid it; and being reclaimed by our Saviour and Redeemer we should live, suffer and die to his honor, so that at all times and especially in the hour of death we may cheerfully and confidently say:

Lord Jesus, for thee I live, for thee I suffer, for thee I die! Lord Jesus, thine will I be in life and death! Grant me, O Lord, eternal salvation! Amen.

THE CONFIRMATION VOW

The Minister says: Beloved sons and daughters, the hour is come in which you are publicly to confess your faith in the Triune God and promise obedience unto your Lord. You may now make confession of the faith upon which you were baptized.

The confirmands repeat the Apostles' Creed.

The Minister continues: I ask you, my friends, before this assembly and in the presence of God, who knows the secrets of all hearts:

1. Do you this day renew the solemn promise made in your name at your baptism, confirming and ratifying the same, and do you desire to be received into the fellowship of the Church of Jesus Christ and to partake of Holy Communion? Then answer: I do.

2. Do you renounce sin and all ungodliness, and do you promise unto your Lord obedience unto death? Then answer: I do.

3. Do you promise with the assistance of the Holy Spirit to live according to the doctrines and precepts of Christ, as presented in the Holy Scriptures, and to remain faithful to the confession of the Evangelical Church? Then answer: I do.

Let us then kneel and pray:

Come, O Holy Spirit, into our hearts, and dwell in us, now and forever. Confirm and establish our promises, and help us to keep them always. Lord Jesus, thou good and gracious Shepherd.

shield us that none of us may go astray. Draw us, O Father, to thy Son, that we may abide with him, and at last inherit everlasting life.   Amen.

THE CONFESSIONAL

Almighty God, Father of our Lord Jesus Christ, I, a poor sinner, acknowlege and bewail my manifold sins and wickedness, which I have from time to time committed against thy holy commandments by thought, word and deed, from unbelief, ingratitude, unfaithfulness, and want of brotherly love; which have marred all my life, provoking against me most justly thy wrath and indignation, in this world and in the world to come. I do earnestly repent, and am heartily sorry for these my transgressions, the remembrance of which is grievous unto me; the burden of them is intolerable. I have no other comfort or trust than thy grace, which aboundeth above my guilt, and the precious merits of my Lord Jesus Christ. Longing after this grace, I say: Father, I have sinned against heaven and in thy sight and am no more worthy to be called thy child; but I come at this time of grace to ask of thee pardon and peace, new confidence toward thee, and strength to lead a new and righteous life through thy good and holy Spirit. Amen.

INDEX OF SCRIPTURE VERSES

A PRAYER FOR THE CHURCH

We thank thee, our Father, for the Church; we praise thee for loving and blessing it. Thou hast been patient with its weaknesses and imperfections; thou hast not allowed its torch to be extinguished; it is still a city, set upon a hill, defended by thy strong arm and prospered by thy grace.

We thank thee for using thy Church as a great channel through which thy blessings unceasingly flow into the ocean of human need, created by our sin, which taints and corrupts our very souls. We praise thee for its service to sinners and saints, to our homeland and the whole world.

Let thy favor ever be upon thy Church; increase our love for it, and give us a growing understanding of its world-wide task. Make it thy voice to our conscience, to keep our feet in the path of duty, and our minds in the love of Christ, our Lord. Amen.